First Edition December 2008 - 5,000 copies
Reprint from January 2010 - April 2014 - 15,000 copies
Reprint June 2016 - 5,000 copies

**Published by:**
**Chinmaya Prakashan**
The Publications Division of
Central Chinmaya Mission Trust
Sandeepany Sadhanalaya
Saki Vihar Road, Powai, Mumbai 400072, India
Tel.: +91-22-2857 2367, 2857 5806  Fax: +91-22-2857 3065
Email: ccmtpublications@chinmayamission.com
Website: www.chinmayamission.com

**Distribution Centre in USA:**
**Chinmaya Mission West**
Publications Division, 560 Bridgetown Pike
Langhorne, PA 19053, USA
Tel.: 1-888-CMW-READ, (215) 396-0390  Fax: (215) 396-9710
Email: publications@chinmayamission.org
Website: www.chinmayapublications.org

Printed by : Parksons Graphics, Mumbai

Book Designed by : Radhika Chopra, Swati Paranjape

Price: ₹ 180/-

ISBN 978-81-7597-444-9

In Indian Culture
# WHY DO WE

Swamini Vimalananda
Radhika Krishnakumar

Illustrations by Vallabh Namshikar

# Foreword

This book is dedicated to the great master
Pujya Gurudev Swami Chinmayanandaji, who
spent his entire life in raising the dignity of Indian
culture and philosophy in the eyes of the world.

Indian culture is admired and respected all over the world for its beauty and depth. This book features in simple terms, the various aspects of both beauty and depth in this culture. Almost every Indian custom and tradition has either a scientific, logical, historical, social or spiritual significance. Understanding this lends meaning to an otherwise mechanical following of the customs, which are often misunderstood to be mere superstitions that fade away in time.

A unique feature of Indian culture is its self-rejuvenating capacity. Customs that are obsolete are gradually dropped as seen in the instances of human sacrifice as well as animal sacrifice to a large extent, sati, untouchability etc. This culture tailors itself constantly to take the best of the modern, technological age without losing its roots.

It is this adaptability that has enabled India to be recognized as one of the world's oldest living civilisations. The customs and traditions selected for these pages are simple, enduring ones that have lasted the test of time and are an integral part of many an Indian home even today.

Pujya Gurudev Swami Chinmayanandaji laid great emphasis on explaining the symbolism in Hindu dharma in a manner that was logical, scientific and appealing to modern man, thereby creating a magnificent cultural renaissance.

# Contents

# WHY DO WE
## light a lamp?

In almost every Indian home a lamp is lit daily before the altar of the Lord. In some houses it is lit at dawn, in some, twice a day – at dawn and dusk – and in a few it is maintained continuously (*akhanda deepa*). All auspicious functions and moments like daily worship, rituals and festivals and even many social occasions like inaugurations commence with the lighting of the lamp, which is often maintained right through the occasion.

## Why do we light a lamp?

Light symbolises knowledge, and darkness ignorance. The Lord is the 'Knowledge Principle' (*chaitanya*) who is the source, the enlivener and the illuminator of all knowledge. Hence light is worshipped as the Lord Himself.

Knowledge removes ignorance just as light removes darkness. Also knowledge is a lasting inner wealth by which all outer achievement can be accomplished. Hence we light the lamp to bow down to knowledge as the greatest of all forms of wealth. Knowledge backs all our actions whether good or bad. We therefore keep a lamp lit during all auspicious occasions as a witness to our thoughts and actions.

Why not light a bulb or tube light? That too would remove darkness. But the traditional oil lamp has a further spiritual significance. The oil or ghee in the lamp symbolises our vaasanas or negative tendencies and the wick, the ego. When lit by spiritual knowledge, the vaasanas get slowly exhausted and the ego too finally perishes. The flame of a lamp always burns upwards. Similarly we should acquire such knowledge as to take us towards higher ideals.

A single lamp can light hundreds more just as a man of knowledge can give it to many more. The brilliance of the light does not diminish despite its repeated use to light many more lamps. So too knowledge does not lessen when shared with or imparted to others. On the contrary it increases in clarity and conviction on giving. It benefits both the receiver and the giver.

Light is self-shining. The Knowledge Principle (*chaitanya*) is self-evident and illumines all without aid.

Whilst lighting the lamp we thus pray:

दीपज्योतिः परब्रह्म दीपः सर्वतमोऽपहः ।
दीपेन साध्यते सर्वं सन्ध्यादीपो नमोऽस्तु ते ॥
..............

deepa-jyotihi parabrahma deepah sarva-tamopahah,
deepena saadhyate sarvam sandhyaa deepo namostute.

I prostrate to the dawn/dusk lamp, whose light is the Knowledge Principle (the Supreme Lord), which removes the darkness of ignorance and by which all can be achieved in life.

Which else shall beautify a home
but the flame of a lovely lamp?
Which else shall adorn the mind
but the light of wisdom deep?
- Swami Chinmayananda

Thus this custom contains a wealth of intellectual and spiritual meaning.

..................

# WHY DO WE

## have a prayer room?

Most Indian homes have a prayer room or altar. A lamp is lit and the Lord worshipped each day. Other spiritual practices like *japa* (repetition of the Lord's name), meditation, *paaraayana* (reading of the scriptures), prayers, devotional singing etc. is also done here. Special worship is done on auspicious occasions like birthdays, anniversaries, festivals and the like. Each member of the family – young or old – communes with and worships the Divine here.

### Why do we have a prayer room?

The Lord is the owner of the entire creation. He is therefore the true owner of the house we live in. We are only the caretakers of His home. The prayer room is the Master room of the house. We are the earthly occupants of His property. This notion rids us of false pride and possessiveness.

But if this attitude of being a caretaker is rather difficult, we

6

could at least think of Him as a very welcome guest. Just as we would house an important guest in the best comfort, so too we felicitate the Lord's presence in our homes by having a prayer room or altar, which is, at all times, kept clean and well-decorated.

Also the Lord is all pervading. To remind us that He resides in our homes with us, we have prayer rooms. Without the grace of the Lord, no task can be successfully or easily accomplished. We invoke His grace by communing with Him in the prayer room each day and on special occasions. Each room in a house is dedicated to a specific function like the bedroom for resting and the drawing room to receive guests. The furniture, decor and the atmosphere of each room are made conducive to the purpose it serves. So too for the purpose of meditation, worship and prayer, we should have a conducive atmosphere – hence the need for a prayer room.

Spiritual thoughts and vibrations accumulated through regular meditation, worship and chanting done there pervade the prayer room and influence the minds of those who spend time there. Even when we are tired or agitated, by just sitting in the prayer room for a while, we feel calm, rejuvenated and spiritually uplifted.

.....................

# WHY DO WE

## do namaste?

Indians greet each other with *namaste*. The two palms are placed together in front of the chest and the head bows whilst saying the word *namaste*. This greeting is for all – people younger than us, of our own age, those older than us, friends and even strangers.

There are five forms of formal traditional greetings enjoined in the scriptures of which *namaskaara* is one. This is understood as prostration but it actually refers to paying homage as we do today when we greet each other with a *namaste*.

## Why do we do *namaste*?

*Namaste* could be just a casual or formal greeting, a cultural convention or an act of worship. However there is much more to it than meets the eye. In Sanskrit *namah + te = namaste*. It means – I bow to you – my greetings, salutations or prostration to you.

*Namah* can also be literally interpreted as *'na mama'* (not mine). It has a spiritual significance of negating or reducing one's ego in the presence of another.

The real meeting between people is the meeting of their minds. When we greet another, we do so with *namaste*, which means, 'may our minds meet', indicated by the folded palms placed before the chest. The bowing down of the head is a gracious form of extending friendship in love and humility.

The spiritual meaning is even deeper. The life force, the divinity, the Self or the Lord in me is the same in all. Recognising this oneness with the meeting of the palms, we salute with head bowed to the Divinity in the person we meet. That is why sometimes, we close our eyes as we do *namaste* to a revered person or the Lord – as if to look within. The gesture is often accompanied by words like 'Ram Ram', 'Jai Shri Krishna', 'Namo Narayana', 'Jai Siya Ram', 'Om Shanti' etc. – indicating the recognition of this divinity.

When we know this significance, our greeting does not remain just a superficial gesture or word but paves the way for a deeper communion with another in an atmosphere of love and respect.

........................

# WHY DO WE

·····································

## prostrate before
## parents and elders?

Indians prostrate to their parents, elders, teachers and noble souls by touching their feet. The elder in turn blesses us by placing his or her hand on or over our heads. Prostration is done daily, when we meet elders and particularly on important occasions like the beginning of a new task, birthdays, festivals etc. In certain traditional circles, prostration is accompanied by *abhivaadana*, which serves to introduce oneself, announce one's family and social stature.

## Why do we offer prostrations?

Man stands on his feet. Touching the feet in prostration is a sign of respect for the age, maturity, nobility and divinity that our elders personify. It symbolises our recognition of their selfless love for us and the sacrifices that they have made for our welfare. It is a way of humbly acknowledging the greatness of another. This tradition reflects the strong family ties, which have been one of India's enduring strengths.

The good wishes (*sankalpa*) and blessings (*aashirvaada*) of elders are highly valued in India. We prostrate to seek them. Good thoughts create positive vibrations. Good wishes springing from a heart full of love, divinity and nobility have a tremendous strength. When we prostrate with humility and respect, we invoke the good wishes and blessings of elders, which flow in the form of positive energy to envelop us. This is why the posture assumed whilst prostrating whether it is in the standing or prone position, enables the entire body to receive the energy thus received.

The different forms of showing respect are:

*Pratyuthana* – rising to welcome a person.
*Namaskaara* – paying homage in the form of *namaste* (discussed separately in this book).
*Upasangrahana* – touching the feet of elders or teachers.
*Saashtaanga* – prostrating fully with the feet, knees, stomach, chest, forehead and arms touching the ground in front of the elder.
*Pratyabhivaadana* – returning a greeting.

Rules are prescribed in our scriptures as to who should prostrate to whom. Wealth, family name, age, moral strength and spiritual knowledge in ascending order of importance qualified men to receive respect. This is why a king though the ruler of the land, would prostrate before a spiritual master. Epics like the *Ramayana* and *Mahabharata* have many stories highlighting this aspect.

This tradition thus creates an environment of mutual love and respect among people ensuring harmony in the family and society.

......................

# WHY DO WE

......................................................

## wear marks
## on the forehead?

Most religious Indians, especially married women wear a *tilak* or *pottu* on the forehead. It is applied daily after a bath and on special occasions, before or after ritualistic worship or a visit to the temple. In many communities, it is enjoined upon married women to sport a *kumkum* mark on their foreheads at all times. The orthodox put it on with due rituals. The *tilak* is applied on saints and images of the Lord as a form of worship and in many parts of North India as a respectful form of welcome, to honour guests or when bidding farewell to a son or husband about to embark on a journey. The *tilak* varies in colour and form.

This custom was not prevalent in the Vedic period. It gained popularity in the *Pauranic* period. Some believe that it originated in South India. In earlier times, the four *varnas* or castes - *Brahmana*, *Kshatriya*, *Vaishya* and *Shudra* – applied different coloured marks.

16

# Why do we wear marks
## (*tilak, pottu* and the like) on the forehead?

The *tilak* or *pottu* invokes a feeling of sanctity in the wearer and others. It is recognized as a religious mark. Its form and colour vary according to one's caste, religious sect or the form of the Lord worshipped.

The *brahmin* applied a white chandan mark signifying purity, as his profession was of a priestly or academic nature. The *kshatriya* applied a red *kumkum* mark signifying valour as he belonged to the warrior races. The *vaishya* wore a yellow *kesar* or turmeric mark signifying prosperity as he was a businessman or trader devoted to creation of wealth. The *shudra* applied a black *bhasma, kasturi* or charcoal mark signifying service as he supported the work of the other three sections. Also Vishnu worshippers apply a *chandan tilak* of the shape of "U", Shiva worshippers a *tripundra* (of the shape of '≡') of *bhasma*, Devi worshippers a red dot of *kumkum* and so on.

The *chandan, kumkum* or *bhasma*, which is offered to the Lord is taken back as *prasaad* and applied on our foreheads. The *tilak* covers the spot between the eyebrows, which is the seat of memory and thinking. It is known as the *aajna chakra* in the language of Yoga. The *tilak* is applied with the prayer – 'May I remember the Lord. May this pious feeling pervade all my activities. May I be righteous in my deeds'. Even when we temporarily forget this prayerful attitude the mark on another reminds us of our resolve. The *tilak* is thus a blessing of the Lord and a protection against wrong tendencies and forces.

The entire body emanates energy in the form of electromagnetic waves – the forehead and the subtle spot between the eyebrows especially so. That is why worry generates heat and causes a headache. The *tilak* or *pottu* cools the forehead, protects us and prevents energy loss. Sometimes the entire forehead is covered with *chandan* or *bhasma*. Using plastic reusable 'sticker bindis' is not very beneficial, even though it serves the purpose of decoration.

This custom is unique to Indians and helps to easily identify us anywhere.

.....................

# WHY DO WE

........................................

## not touch papers, books and people with the feet?

In Indian homes, we are taught from a very young age never to touch papers, books and people with our feet. If the feet accidentally touch papers, books, musical instruments or any other educational equipment, children are told to reverentially touch what was stamped with their hands and then touch their eyes as a mark of apology.

Why do we not touch papers and people with the feet?

To Indians, knowledge is sacred and divine. So it must be given respect at all times. Nowadays we separate subjects as sacred and secular. But in ancient India every subject – academic or spiritual – was considered divine and taught by the *Guru* in the *gurukula*.

The custom of not stepping on educational tools is a frequent reminder of the high position accorded to knowledge in

Indian culture. Thus knowledge, a knowledgeable person, learning materials, the source of knowledge and the deity of knowledge, all are considered worshipful From an early age, this wisdom fosters in us a deep reverence for books and education. This is also the reason why we worship books, vehicles and instruments once a year on *Sarasvati Pooja* or *Ayudha Pooja* day, dedicated to the Goddess of Learning. So, each day before starting our studies, we pray:

सरस्वति नमस्तुभ्यं वरदे कामरूपिणी ।
विद्यारंभं करिष्यामि सिद्धिर्भवतु मे सदा ॥
.............

sarasvati namas-tubhyam varade kaama roopini,
vidyaarambham karishyaami sidhir-bhavatu me sadaa.

O Goddess Sarasvati, the giver of
boons and fulfiller of wishes,
I prostrate to You before starting my studies.
May You always fulfill me.

Children are also strongly discouraged from touching people with their feet. Even if this happens accidentally, we touch the person and bring the fingers to our eyes as a mark of apology. Even when elders touch a younger person inadvertently with their feet, they immediately apologize.

To touch another with the feet is considered an act of misdemeanor. Why is this so?

Man is regarded as the most beautiful, living, breathing temple of the Lord! Therefore touching another with the feet is akin to disrespecting the divinity within him or her. This calls for an immediate apology, which is offered with reverence and humility.

Thus, many of our customs are designed to be simple but powerful reminders or pointers of profound philosophical truths. This is one of the factors that has kept Indian culture alive across centuries.

......................

# WHY DO WE

## apply the holy ash?

The ash of any burnt object is not regarded as holy ash. *Bhasma* (the holy ash) is the ash from the *homa* (sacrificial fire) where special wood along with *ghee* (clarified butter) and other herbs is offered as worship of the Lord. Or the deity is worshipped by pouring ash as *abhisheka* and is then distributed as *bhasma*.

*Bhasma* is generally applied on the forehead. Some apply it on certain parts of the body like the upper arms, chest etc. Some ascetics rub it all over the body. Many consume a pinch of it each time they receive it.

### Why do we use *bhasma*?

The application of *bhasma* signifies destruction of the evil and remembrance of the divine. *Bha - bhartsanam* (to destroy) and *sma - smaranam* (to remember). *Bhasma* is called *vibhuti* (which means 'glory') as it gives glory to one who applies it and *raksha* (which means protection) as it protects the wearer from ill health and evil, by purifying him or her.

*Homa* (offering of oblations into the fire with sacred chants) signifies the offering or surrender of the ego and egocentric desires into the flame of knowledge for a noble and selfless cause. The consequent ash signifies the purity of the mind, which results from such actions. Also the fire of knowledge burns the oblation and wood signifying ignorance and inertia respectively. The ash we apply indicates that we should burn false identification with the body and become free of the limitations of birth and death. The application of ash also reminds us that the body is perishable and shall one day be reduced to ashes. We should therefore not get too attached to it. Death can come at any moment and this awareness must increase our drive to make the best use of time.

*Bhasma* is specially associated with Lord Shiva who applies it all over His body. Shiva devotees apply *bhasma* as a *tripundra* (the form of ' ≡ '). When applied with a red spot in the centre, the mark symbolizes Shiva-Shakti (the unity of energy and matter that creates the entire seen and unseen universe).

Ash is what remains when all the wood is burnt away and it does not decay. Similarly, the Lord is the imperishable

Truth that remains when the entire creation of innumerable names and forms is dissolved.

*Bhasma* has medicinal value and is used in many ayurvedic medicines. The *Upanishads* say that the famous *Mrutyunjaya mantra* should be chanted whilst applying ash on the forehead.

त्र्यंबकं यजामहे सुगन्धिं पुष्टिवर्धनम् ।
उर्वारुकमिव बन्धनान्मृत्योर्मुक्षीय माऽमृतात् ॥

.............

tryambakam yajaamahe sugandhim pushtivardhanam,
urvaa rukamiva bandhanaan mrytyor muksheeyamaa
amrutaat

We worship the three-eyed Lord Shiva who nourishes
and spreads fragrance in our lives. May He free us from
the shackles of sorrow, change and death — effortlessly,
like the fall of a ripe cucumber from its stem and bestow
immortality.

.....................

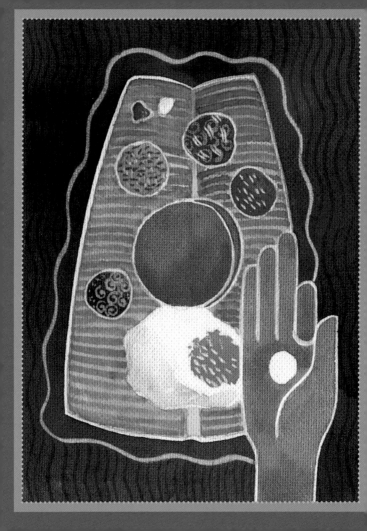

# WHY DO WE

## offer food to the Lord
## before eating it?

In western tradition food is partaken after a thanksgiving prayer – grace. Indians make an offering of it to the Lord and later partake of it as *prasaada* – a holy gift from the Lord. In temples and in many homes, the cooked food is first offered to the Lord each day. The offered food is mixed with the rest of the food and then served as *prasaada*. In our daily ritualistic worship *(pooja)* too we offer *naivedyam* (food) to the Lord.

### Why do we offer *naivedya*?

The Lord is omnipotent and omniscient. All that we do is by His strength and knowledge alone. Being the totality, all that we receive in life as a result of our actions is really His alone. We acknowledge this through the act of offering food to Him. This is exemplified by the famous *aarti* words in Hindi- *tera tujhko arpan* – 'I offer what is Yours to You'. Thereafter what is received is His gift to us *(prasaada)*, graced by His divine touch.

Knowing this, our entire attitude to food and the act of eating changes. The food offered is pure and the best and shared with others, before consuming. We do not demand, complain or criticise the quality of the food we get. We do not waste or reject it. We eat it with a cheerful acceptance *(prasaada buddhi)*. When we become established in this attitude, we are then able to cheerfully accept all we get in life as His *prasaada*.

Before we partake of our daily meals we first sprinkle water around the plate as an act of purification. Five morsels of food are placed on the side of the plate acknowledging the debt owed by us to: a) Divine forces *(devata runa)* - for their benign grace and protection. b) Our ancestors *(pitru runa)* - for giving us their lineage and a family culture. c) The Sages *(rishi runa)* - as our religion and culture have been 'realised', maintained and handed down to us by them. d) Our fellow beings *(manushya runa)* - who constitute the society, without the support of which we could not live as we do. e) Other living beings *(bhuta runa)* - for serving us selflessly.

Thereafter the Lord, the life force, who is also within us as the five life-giving physiological functions, is offered the food. This is done with the chant – *Om praanaaya swaahaa, Om apaanaaya swaahaa, Om vyaanaaya swaahaa, Om udaanaaya swaahaa, Om samaanaaya swaahaa, Om brahmane swaahaa* [referring to the five physiological functions – respiratory (*praana*), excretory (*apaana*), circulatory (*vyaana*), digestive (*samaana*) and reversal (*udaana*) systems]. After offering the food thus, it is eaten as *prasaada* – blessed food.

To remember this concept, many chant following verses of the Geeta.

ब्रह्मार्पणं ब्रह्महविः ब्रह्माग्नौ ब्रह्मणाहुतम् ।
ब्रह्मैव तेन गन्तव्यं ब्रह्मकर्मसमाधिना ॥
अहं वैश्वानरो भूत्वा प्राणिनां देहमाश्रितः ।
प्राणापान समायुक्तः पचाम्यन्नं चतुर्विधम् ॥
.............

brahmaarpanam brahmahavihi brahmaagnau brahmanaahutam,
    brahmaiva tena gantavyam brahmakarma samaadhina.
 aham vaishvaanaro bhootvaa praaninaam dehamaashritah,
praanaapaana samaayuktah pachaamyannam chaturvidham.

Brahman is the oblation; the clarified butter; the fire; the oblation... Brahman (the Supreme) shall be reached by him, who sees the Supreme in all actions. Residing in all living beings as the digestive fire, I digest the four types of food eaten by them (as an offering to Me).

# WHY DO WE
## do pradakshina?

When we visit a temple, after offering prayers, we circumambulate the *sanctum sanctorum* with folded hands often chanting prayers. This is called *pradakshina*.

## Why do we do *pradakshina*?

We cannot draw a circle without a centre point. The Lord is the centre, source and essence of our lives. Recognising Him as the focal point in our lives, we go about doing our daily chores. This is the significance of *pradakshina*.

Also every point on the circumference of a circle is equidistant from the centre. This means that wherever or whoever we may be, we are equally close to the Lord. His grace flows towards us without partiality.

## Why is *pradakshina* done only in a clockwise manner?

The reason is not, as a person said, to avoid a traffic jam! As we do *pradakshina*, the Lord is always on our right. In India the right side symbolises auspiciousness. It is a telling fact that even in the English language it is called the 'right' side and not the wrong one! So as we circumambulate the *sanctum sanctorum* we remind ourselves to lead an auspicious life of righteousness, with the Lord who is the indispensable source of help and strength, as our guide -the 'right hand' – the *dharma* aspect – of our lives. We thereby overcome our wrong tendencies and avoid repeating the sins of the past.

Indian scriptures enjoin – *matrudevo bhava, pitrudevo bhava, acharyadevo bhava*. 'May you consider your mother, father and teachers as you would the Lord'. With this in mind we also do *pradakshina* around our parents and divine personages. The story of Lord Ganesha beating his brother Lord Kartikeya in a race to circumambulate the world by going around his parents is a well-known one. Sacred mountains (*giri pradakshina* of Tiruvenamalai) and holy rivers (Narmada *parikrama*) are also circumabulated.

After the completion of traditional worship (*pooja*), we customarily do *pradakshina* with folded hands around ourselves. In this way we recognize and remember the Supreme divinity within us, which alone is idolised in the form of the Lord that we worship outside.

As we circumambulate, we chant:

यानि कानि च पापानि जन्मान्तरकृतानि च ।
तानि तानि विनश्यन्ति प्रदक्षिणपदे पदे ॥

.............

yaani kaani cha paapaani
janmaantara kritaani cha,
taani taani vinashyanti
pradakshina pade pade.

All the sins committed by an individual from
innumerable past births are destroyed by each
step taken whilst doing *pradakshina*.

.....................

# WHY DO WE

## regard trees and plants as sacred?

From ancient times, Indians have worshipped plants and trees and regarded all flora and fauna as sacred. This is not an old-fashioned or uncivilised practice. It reveals the sensitivity, foresight and refinement of Indian culture. While modern man often works to 'conquer' Mother Nature, ancient Indians 'worshipped' her.

### Why do we regard plants and trees as sacred?

The Lord, the life in us, pervades all living beings, be they plants or animals. Hence, they are all regarded as sacred. Human life on earth depends on plants and trees. They give us the vital factors that make life possible on earth: food, oxygen, clothing, shelter, medicines etc. They lend beauty to our surroundings. They serve man without expectation and sacrifice themselves to sustain him. They epitomise sacrifice. If a stone is thrown on a fruit-laden tree, the tree in turn showers its fruits!

In fact, the flora and fauna owned the earth before man appeared on it. Presently, the world is seriously threatened by the destruction of forestlands and the extinction of many species of vegetation due to man's callous attitude towards them. We protect only what we value. Hence, in India, we are taught to regard trees and plants as sacred. Naturally, we will then protect them.

Indian scriptures tell us to plant ten trees if for any reason, we have to cut one. We are advised to use parts of trees and plants only as much as is needed for food, fuel, shelter etc. We are also urged to apologise to a plant or tree before cutting it to avoid incurring a specific sin named *soona*. In our childhood, we are told stories of the sacrifice and service done by plants and trees and about our duty to plant and nourish them. Certain *saatvic* trees and plants like *tulasi* and *peepal*, which have tremendous beneficial qualities, are worshipped till today.

It is believed that divine beings manifest as trees and plants, and many people worship them to fulfill their desires or to please the Lord.

......................

# WHY DO WE

## ring the bell in a temple?

In most temples there are one or more bells hung from the top, near the entrance. The devotee rings the bell as soon as he enters, thereafter proceeding for *darshan* of the Lord and prayers. Children love jumping up or being carried high in order to reach the bell.

### Why do we ring the bell?

Is it to wake up the Lord? But the Lord never sleeps. Is it to let the Lord know we have come? He does not need to be told, as He is all knowing. Is it a form of seeking permission to enter His precinct? Since the temple is like a homecoming no permission for entering is needed. The Lord welcomes us at all times. Then why do we ring the bell?

The ringing of the bell produces an auspicious sound. There should be auspiciousness within and without, to gain the vision of the Lord who is all-auspiciousness. The ringing

produces the sound *'Om'*, which is the universal name of the Lord.

Even while doing the ritualistic *aarati*, we ring the bell. It is sometimes accompanied by the auspicious sounds of the conch and other musical instruments. An added significance of ringing the bell, conch and other instruments is that they help drown any inauspicious or irrelevant noises and comments that might disturb or distract the worshippers in their devotional ardour, concentration and inner peace.

As we start the daily ritualistic worship (*pooja*) we ring the bell, chanting:

आगमार्थं तु देवानां गमनार्थं तु रक्षसाम् ।
कुर्वे घण्टारवं तत्र देवताह्वान लक्षणम् ॥

.............

aagamaartham tu devaanaam
gamanaartham tu rakshasaam,
kurve ghantaaravam tatra
devataahvaahna lakshanam.

I ring this bell indicating the invocation of divinity, so that virtuous and noble forces enter (my home and heart); and the demonic and evil forces from within and without, depart.

# WHY DO WE
·····································
## fast?

Most devout Indians fast regularly or on special occasions like festivals. On such days they do not eat at all, eat once or may do with fruits or a special diet of simple food. Some undertake rigorous fasts when they do not even drink water the whole day! Fasting is done for many reasons – to please the Lord, to discipline oneself and even to protest. Gandhiji fasted to protest against the British rule.

### Why do we fast?

Is it to save food or to create an appetite to feast after the fast? Not really. Then why do we fast?

Fasting in Sanskrit is called *upavaasa. Upa* means 'near' + *vaasa* means 'to stay'. *Upavaasa* therefore means staying near (the Lord), meaning the attainment of close mental proximity with the Lord. Then what has *upavaasa* to do with food? A lot of our time and energy is spent in procuring food items, preparing, cooking, eating and digesting food. Certain food types make our minds dull and agitated. Hence on certain days man decides to save time and conserve his energy by eating either simple, light food or totally abstaining from eating so that his mind becomes alert and pure.

The mind, otherwise pre-occupied by the thought of food, now entertains noble thoughts and stays with the Lord. Since it is a self-imposed form of discipline (*tapas*) it is usually adhered to with joy.

One usually takes up a vow (*vrat*) of fasting. To keep a promise strengthens our will and confidence. Also every machine or system needs a break and an overhaul to work at its best. Rest and a change of diet during fasting are very good for the digestive system and the entire body.

The more you indulge the senses, the more they make their demands. Fasting helps us to cultivate control over our senses, sublimate our desires and guide our minds to be poised and at peace.

Fasting should not make us weak, irritable or create an urge to indulge later. This happens when there is no noble goal behind fasting. Some fast, rather they diet, merely to reduce weight. To keep the body trim by dieting, only achieves physical well being. Fasting gives it a spiritual connotation of dieting for a higher cause - as a vow to please the Lord or to fulfill their desires, to develop will power, control the senses or as a form of austerity. The *Bhagavad Geeta* urges us to eat appropriately – neither too less nor too much – *yukta-aahaara* and to eat simple, pure and healthy food (a *saatvik* diet) even when not fasting.

......................

# WHY DO WE

## worship the kalasha?

First of all what is a *kalasha*? A brass, mud or copper pot is filled with water. Mango leaves are placed in the mouth of the pot and a coconut is placed over it. A red or white thread is tied around the neck of the pot or sometimes all around it in an intricate diamond-shaped pattern. The pot may be decorated with designs. Such a pot is known as a *kalasha*. When the pot is filled with water or rice, it is known as *poorna kumbha* representing the inert body which when filled with the divine life force gains the power to do all the wonderful things that makes life what it is.

A *kalasha* is placed with due rituals on all important occasions like the traditional house warming (*grahapravesha*), wedding and daily worship. It is placed near the entrance as a sign of welcome. It is also used in a traditional manner while receiving holy personages.

Why do we worship the *kalasha*?

Before the creation came into being, Lord Vishnu was reclining on His snake-bed in the milky ocean. From His navel emerged a lotus from which appeared Lord Brahma, the Creator, who thereafter created this world. The water in the *kalasha* symbolises the primordial water from which the entire creation emerged. It is the giver of life to all and has the potential of creating innumerable names and forms, the inert objects and the sentient beings and all that is auspicious in the world. It symbolises the creative energy behind the universe.

The leaves and coconut represent creation. The thread represents the love that 'binds' all in creation. The *kalasha* is therefore considered auspicious and worshipped.

The waters from all the holy rivers, the knowledge of all the Vedas and the blessings of all the deities are invoked in the *kalasha* and prayers are offered to herald nourishment, prosperity and peace. Its water is thereafter used for all the rituals, including the *abhisheka* – the ritualistic bath given to the Lord. The consecration (*kumbhaabhisheka*) of a temple is done in a grand manner with elaborate rituals including the pouring of one or more *kalashas* of holy water on the top of the temple. The waters of the *kalasha* are also sprinkled over the heads of the devotees as a blessing and around the house after rituals to sanctify all.

When the *asuras* (demons) and the *devas* (divine beings) churned the milky ocean, the Lord appeared bearing the pot of *amrita* (nectar), which had the power to bestow everlasting life. Thus the *kalasha* also symbolises immortality.

Men of wisdom are full and complete as they identify with the infinite Truth (*poornatvam*). They brim with joy and love and represent all that is auspicious. We greet them with a *poorna kumbha* (full pot) acknowledging their greatness and as a sign of respectful and reverential welcome, with a 'full heart'.

......................

# WHY DO WE

## worship tulasi?

Either in the front, back or central courtyard of most Indian homes there is a *tulasi matham* – an altar bearing a *tulasi* plant. In the present day apartments too, many maintain a potted *tulasi* plant. The lady of the house lights a lamp, waters the plant, worships and circumambulates it. The stem, leaves, seeds and even the soil, which provides it a base, are considered holy. A *tulasi* leaf is always placed in the food offered to the Lord. It is also offered to the Lord during *poojas*, especially to Lord Vishnu and His Incarnations.

### Why do we worship the *tulasi*?

In Sanskrit *talasi* is that which is incomparable (in its qualities) - *tulanaa naasti athaiva tulasi*. For Indians it is one of the most sacred plants. In fact it is known to be the only thing used in the ritualistic worship (*pooja*), which, once used, can be washed and reused again – as it is considered self-purifying.

As one story goes, Tulasi was the devoted wife of Shankhachuda, a celestial being. She believed that Lord Krishna tricked her into sinning. So she cursed Him to become a stone (*shaaligraama*). Seeing her devotion and adherence to righteousness, the Lord blessed her saying that she would become the worshipped plant, *tulasi* that would adorn His head. He also declared that all offerings would be incomplete without the *tulasi* leaf – hence the worship of tulasi.

She also symbolises Goddess Lakshmi, the consort of Lord Vishnu. Those who wish to be righteous and have a happy family life worship the *tulasi*. Tulasi is married to the Lord with all pomp and show as in any wedding. This is because, according to another legend, the Lord blessed her that she would be His consort.

Satyabhama once tried to weigh Lord Krishna with her legendary wealth. The scales did not balance even with her entire wealth. Finally Rukmini placed a single *tulasi* leaf along with the wealth on the scale. Her devoted offering of the sacred *tulasi* balanced the scales. Thus the *tulasi* played the vital role of demonstrating to the world that even a small object offered with devotion means more to the Lord than all the wealth in the world. It also shows that anything endowed with righteousness becomes invaluable.

The *tulasi* leaf has great medicinal value and is used to cure various ailments, including the common cold.

यन्मूले सर्व तीर्थानि यदग्रे सर्व देवता ।
यन्मध्ये सर्व वेदाश्च तुलसी तां नमाम्यहम् ॥

..............

yanmule sarva teerthaani
yadagre sarva devataa,
yanmadhye sarva vedaascha
tulasi taam namamyaham.

I bow down to the *tulasi*,
at whose base are all the holy places,
at whose top reside all the deities and
in whose middle are all the *Vedas*.

.....................

# WHY DO WE

## consider the lotus as special?

The lotus is India's national flower and rightly so. Not long ago, the lakes and ponds of India were full of many hued lotuses.

## Why do we consider the lotus special?

The lotus is the symbol of truth, auspiciousness and beauty (*satyam, shivam, sundaram*). The Lord is also of that nature and therefore, His various aspects are compared to a lotus (lotus-eyes, lotus feet, lotus hands, the lotus of the heart etc.). Our scriptures and ancient literature extol the beauty of the lotus. Art and architecture also portray the lotus in various decorative motifs and paintings. Many people have names of or related to the lotus: Padma, Pankaja, Kamal, Kamala, Kamalaakshi etc. The Goddess of wealth, Lakshmi sits on a lotus and carries one in Her hand.

The lotus blooms with the rising sun and closes at night.

Similarly, our minds open up and expand with the light of knowledge. The lotus grows even in slushy areas. It remains beautiful and untainted despite its surroundings, reminding us that we too can and should strive to remain pure and beautiful within, under all circumstances. The lotus leaf never gets wet even though it is always in water. It symbolises the man of wisdom (*gnaani*) who remains ever joyous, unaffected by the world of sorrow and change. This is revealed in a *shloka* from the *Bhagavad Geeta* :

ब्रह्मण्याधाय कर्माणि सङ्गं त्यक्त्वा करोति यः ।
लिप्यते न स पापेन पद्मपत्रमिवाम्भसा ॥

.............

brahmanyaadhaaya karmaani
sangam tyaktvaa karoti yaha,
lipyate na sa paapena
padma patram ivaambhasaa.

He who does actions, offering them to *Brahman*
(the Supreme), abandoning attachment,
is not tainted by sin, just as a lotus leaf
remains unaffected by the water on it.

From this, we learn that what is natural to the man of wisdom becomes a discipline to be practised by all spiritual seekers and devotees (*saadhakas*).

Our bodies have certain energy centres described in the *Yoga Shaastras* as *chakras*. Each one is associated with a lotus with a certain number of petals. For example, the *Sahasra chakra* at the top of the head, which opens when the yogi attains Godhood or Realisation, is represented by a lotus with a thousand petals. Also, the lotus posture (*padmaasana*) is recommended when one sits for meditation.

A lotus emerged from the navel of Lord Vishnu. Lord Brahma originated from it to create the world. Hence, the lotus symbolises the link between the Creator and the Supreme Cause. It also symbolises *Brahmaloka*, the abode of Lord Brahma.

The auspicious sign of the *swastika* is said to have evolved from the lotus.

From the above, we can well appreciate why the lotus is India's national flower and is so special to Indians.

.....................

# WHY DO WE
## blow the conch?

In temples or at homes, the conch is blown once or several times before ritualistic worship (*pooja*). It is sometimes blown whilst doing *aarati* or to mark an auspicious occasion. It is blown before a battle starts or to announce the victory of an army. It is also placed in the altar and worshipped.

### Why do we blow the conch?

When the conch is blown, the primordial sound of *Om* emanates. *Om* is an auspicious sound that was chanted by the Lord before creating the world. It represents the world and the Truth behind it.

As the story goes, the demon Shankhaasura defeated the devas, stole the Vedas and went to the bottom of the ocean. The *devās* appealed to Lord Vishnu for help. He incarnated as *Matsya Avataara* - the 'fish incarnation' and killed Shankhaasura. The Lord blew the conch-shaped bone of his ear and head. The conch therefore is known as *shankha* after Shankhaasura.

The *Om* sound emanated from the conch blown by the Lord. And from *Om* emerged the Vedas. All knowledge enshrined in the Vedas is an elaboration of *Om*. The conch blown by the Lord is called Paanchajanya. He carries it at all times in one of His four hands. It represents *dharma* or righteousness that is one of the four goals (*purushaarthas*) of life. The sound of the conch is thus also the victory call of good over evil. If we place a conch close to our ears, we hear the sound of the waves of the ocean.

Another well-known purpose of blowing the conch and other instruments, known traditionally to produce auspicious sounds is to drown or mask negative comments or noises that may disturb or upset the atmosphere or the minds of worshippers.

Ancient India lived in her villages. Each village was presided over by a primary temple and several smaller ones. During the aarati performed after all important poojas and on sacred occasions, the conch used to be blown. Since villages were generally small, the sound of the conch would be heard all over the village. People who could not make it to the temple were reminded to stop whatever they were doing, at least for a few seconds, and mentally bow to the Lord. The conch sound served to briefly elevate people's' minds to a prayerful attitude even in the middle of their busy daily routine.

The conch is placed at the altar in temples and homes next to the Lord as a symbol of *Naada Brahma* (Truth), the Vedas, Om, *dharma*, victory and auspiciousness. It is often used to offer devotees *thirtha* (sanctified water) to raise their minds to the highest Truth.

It is worshipped with the following verse:

त्वं पुरा सागरोत्पन्नः विष्णुना विधृतः करे ।
देवैश्च पूजितः सर्वैः पाञ्चजन्य नमोऽस्तु ते ॥

............

tvam puraa saagarotpannah vishnunaa vidhrutah kare,
devaischa poojitah sarvaihi, paanchajanya namostu te.

Salutations to *Paanchajanya*,
the conch born of the ocean,
held in the hand of Lord Vishnu
and worshipped by all the *devas*.

....................

# WHY DO WE
## say shaanti thrice?

*Shaanti*, meaning 'peace', is a natural state of being. Disturbances are created either by us or others. For example, peace already exists in a place until someone makes noise. When agitations end, peace which underlies all agitations is experienced, since it was already there. Where there is peace, there is happiness. Therefore, every one without exception desires peace in his or her life. However, peace within or without seems very hard to attain. A rare few manage to remain peaceful within, even in the midst of external agitation and troubles. To invoke peace, we chant prayers. By chanting prayers peace is experienced internally, irrespective of the external disturbances. All peace-invoking prayers end by chanting shaanti thrice.

### Why do we say *shaanti* thrice?

It is believed that *trivaaram satyam* – that which is said thrice comes true. For emphasizing a point we repeat a thing thrice. In the court of law also, one who takes the witness stand says, "I shall speak the truth, the whole truth and nothing but the truth". We chant *shaanti* thrice to emphasize our intense desire for peace.

All obstacles, problems and sorrows originate from three sources:

1. *Aadhidaivika*: The unseen divine forces over which we have little or no control like earthquakes, floods and volcanic eruptions.
2. *Aadhibhautika*: The known factors around us like accidents, human contacts, pollution and crime.
3. *Aadhyaatmika*: Problems of our bodies and minds like diseases, anger and frustrations.

We sincerely pray to the Lord that at least while we undertake special tasks or even in our daily lives, there are no problems or that, problems are minimised from the three sources written about above. May peace alone prevail. Hence shaanti is chanted thrice. It is chanted aloud the first time, addressing the unseen forces. It is chanted softer the second time directed to our immediate surroundings and those around, and softest the last time as it is addressed to oneself.

......................

# WHY DO WE
## chant Om?

*Om* is one of the most chanted sound symbols in India. It has a profound effect on the body and mind of the one who chants and also on the surroundings. Most manträs and vedic prayers start with *Om*. All auspicious actions begin with *Om*. It is even used as a greeting – *Om, Hari Om* etc. It is repeated as a mantra or meditated upon. Its form is worshipped, contemplated upon or used as an auspicious sign.

## Why do we chant Om?

*Om* is the universal name of the Lord. It is made up of the letters 'A' (phonetically as in 'around'), 'U' (phonetically as in 'put') and 'M' (phonetically as in 'mum'). The sound emerging from the vocal chords starts from the base of the throat as 'A'. With the coming together of the lips, 'U' is formed and when the lips are closed, all sound ends in 'M'. The three letters symbolise the three states (waking, dream and deep sleep), the three deities (Brahma, Vishnu and Shiva), the three

Vedas (*Rig*, *Yajur* and *Sama*), the three worlds (*Bhuh*, *Bhuvah*, *Suvah*) etc. The Lord is all these and beyond. The formless, attributeless Lord (Brahman) is represented by the silence between two *Om* chants. *Om* is also called pranava meaning - '(symbol or sound) that by which the Lord is praised'. The entire essence of the Vedas is enshrined in the word *Om*.

It is said that the Lord started creating the world after chanting *Om* and *atha*. Hence these sounds are considered to create an auspicious beginning for any task that we undertake.

The *Om* chant should have the resounding sound of a bell (aaooommm). It fills the mind with peace, makes it focused and replete with subtle sound. People meditate on its meaning and attain realisation.

*Om* is written in different ways in different places. The most common form (ॐ) symbolises Lord Ganesha. The upper curve is the head; the lower large one, the stomach; the side one, the trunk; and the semi-circular mark with the dot, the sweet-meat ball (*modaka*) in Lord Ganesha's hand.

Thus *Om* symbolises everything – the means and the goal of life, the world and the Truth behind it, the material and the Sacred, all forms and the Formless.

# WHY DO WE

## offer a coconut?

In India one of the most common offerings in a temple is a coconut. It is also offered on occasions like weddings, festivals, the use of a new vehicle, bridge, house etc. A pot (*kalasha*) full of water, adorned with mango leaves and a coconut on top is worshipped on important occasions and used to receive revered guests.

It is offered in the sacrificial fire whilst performing *homa*. The coconut is broken and placed before the Lord. It is later distributed as *prasaada*.

## Why do we offer a coconut?

It is offered to please the Lord or to fulfill our desires. There was a time when animal sacrifice (*bali*) was practised, symbolising the offering of our animalistic tendencies to the Lord. Slowly this practice faded and the coconut was offered instead. The fibre covering of the dried coconut is removed all over, except for a tuft on the top. The marks on the coconut make it look like the head of a human being. The coconut is broken, symbolising the breaking of the ego. The juice within, representing the inner tendencies (*vaasanas*) is offered along with the white kernel – the mind, to the Lord. A mind thus purified by the touch of the Lord is used as *prasaada* (a holy gift).

In the traditional *abhisheka* ritual, done in all temples and many homes, several materials are poured over the deity like milk, curd, honey, tender coconut water, sandal paste, holy ash etc. Each material has a specific significance of bestowing certain benefits on worshippers. Tender coconut water is used in abhisheka rituals since it is believed to bestow spiritual growth on the seeker.

The coconut also symbolises selfless service. Every part of the tree – the trunk, leaves, fruit, coir etc. is used in innumerable ways like thatched roofs, mats, tasty dishes, oil, soap etc.

The coconut tree takes in even salty water from the earth and converts it into sweet nutritive water that is especially beneficial to sick people. It is used in the preparation of many Ayurvedic medicines and in other alternative medicinal systems.

The marks on the coconut are even thought to represent the three-eyed Lord Shiva and therefore it is considered to be a means to fulfill our desires. In certain rituals a coconut is placed on a *kalasha* decorated, garlanded and worshipped as symbolic of Lord Shiva and of the man of Realisation (*jnaani*).

......................

# WHY DO WE
## do aarati?

Towards the end of every ritualistic worship of the Lord (*pooja*) or devotional singing (*bhajan*) or to welcome an honoured guest or saint, we perform the *aarati*. This is always accompanied by the ringing of the bell and sometimes by singing, playing of musical instruments and clapping.

It is one of the sixteen steps (*shodasha upachaara*) of the *pooja* ritual. It is referred to as the offering of the auspicious light (*mangala niraajanam*). Holding the lighted lamp in the right hand, we wave the flame in a clockwise circling movement to light the entire form of the Lord. As the light is waved we either do mental or loud chanting of prayers or simply behold the beautiful form of the Lord, illumined by the lamp. We experience an added intensity in our prayers and the Lord's image seems to manifest a special beauty at that time.

At the end of the *aarati* we place our hands over the flame and then gently touch our eyes and the top of the head. We have seen and participated in this ritual from our childhood.

## Why do we do the *aarati?*

Having worshipped the Lord with love – performing *abhisheka*, decorating the image and offering fruits and delicacies, whilst performing the *aarti* we see the beauty of the Lord in all His glory. Our mind gets focused on each limb of the Lord illumined by the light of the *aarti*. It is akin to silent open-eyed meditation on His beautiful form. The singing, clapping, ringing of the bell etc. denote the joy and auspiciousness, which accompanies the vision of the Lord.

*Aarati* is often performed with camphor. This holds a telling spiritual significance. Camphor, when lit burns itself out completely. It represents our inherent tendencies (*vaasanas*).

Lit by the fire of knowledge, which illumines the Lord (Truth), our *vaasanas* and the ego, which creates a sense of individuality that keeps us separate from the Lord, burn themselves out completely. Also even as it burns and sacrifices itself, the lighted camphor reveals the glory of the Lord and emits a pleasant fragrance. Similarly we too should willingly sacrifice ourselves and all we have as we serve the

Guru and society and spread the fragrance of love to all.

When the *aarati* is actually performed quite often our eyes close automatically. This is to signify that each of us is a temple of the Lord - we hold the divinity within. The priest reveals the form of the Lord clearly with the *aarati* flame. The Guru too clearly reveals to us the divinity within us with the light of spiritual knowledge.

At the end of the *aarati*, we place our hands over the flame and then touch our eyes and the top of the head. It means – may the light that illumined the Lord light up my vision; may my vision be divine and my thoughts noble and beautiful.

The philosophical meaning of *aarati* extends further. The sun, moon, stars, lightning and fire are the natural sources of light. The Lord is the source of all these wondrous phenomena of the universe. It is due to Him alone that all else exists and shines. As we light up the Lord with the flame of the *aarati*, we turn our attention to the very source of all light, which symbolises knowledge and life.

Also the sun, moon and fire are the respective presiding deities of the intellect, mind and speech. The Lord is the supreme Consciousness that illumines all of them. Without Him the intellect cannot think, the mind cannot feel or the tongue speak. The Lord is beyond the mind, intellect and speech. How can these finite equipments illumine the infinite Lord?

Therefore as we perform the *aarati* we chant:

न तत्र सूर्यो भाति न चन्द्रतारकम्
नेमा विद्युतो भान्ति कुतोऽयमग्निः।
तमेव भान्तमनुभाति सर्वम्
तस्य भासा सर्वमिदं विभाति॥

.............

na tatra suryo bhati na chandra taarakam
nemaa vidyuto bhaanti kutoyamagnih,
tameva bhantam anubhaati sarvam
tasya bhaasa sarvam idam vibhaati.

He is there where the sun does not shine, nor the moon, stars and lightning. Then what to talk of this small flame (in my hand)! Everything (in the universe) shines only after the Lord And by His light alone is all illumined.

.................

शान्तिः
शान्तिः
शान्तिः